"As with all of Sa[...] d a Happy Marriage eclipses the theatrical genre and becomes something very much its own. Its characters are fully actualized; they are funny without being caricatures, and their complexity helps each one to forge new and necessary modern archetypes. The play itself is compulsively readable and asks to be returned to over and over again; each reading reveals totally fresh revelations. A play (on its surface) about polyamory, *How to Transcend a Happy Marriage* shows the depths of relationships that exist outside the standard romantic narrative, and illuminates all that is brutal, funny, and beautiful about this kind of loving. It was easily my favorite play of the past ten years."

—Sophie Lucido Johnson, author,
Many Love: A Memoir of Polyamory and Finding Love(s)

"An intriguing new comedy . . . Polyamory complicates things (think of the logistics!) but also satisfies the human animal's omnivorous nature and spiritual longing to be part of something bigger. Striving for transcendence, George discovers, to her surprise and ours, that magic and meaning were in the neighborhood all along."

—Zac Thompson, *Village Voice*

"I have been in the audience of many of Sarah's plays and she continues to be a pertinent observer of the intricacies of intimate relationships and the interplay with sexuality."

—Esther Perel, MA, LMFT,
master trainer, therapist, speaker; author,
Mating in Captivity: Unlocking Erotic Intelligence

"Ruhl has one of the liveliest intellects of any playwright today."

—Jeremy Gerard, *Deadline*

"Sexy and smart . . . Ruhl approaches polyamory with her usual wit and intelligence, subtly questioning our societal assumptions around love and commitment even as she makes us feel as comfortable as honored guests in her home."

—Zachary Stewart, *TheaterMania*

"Provocative and enlightening."

—Robert Hofler, *Wrap*

How to transcend

a happy marriage

How to transcend

a happy marriage

By Sarah Ruhl

THEATRE COMMUNICATIONS GROUP
NEW YORK
2019

The publication of *How to transcend a happy marriage*, through TCG's Book Program, is made possible in part by the New York State Council on the Arts with the support of Governor Andrew Cuomo and the New York State Legislature.

TCG books are exclusively distributed to the book trade by Consortium Book Sales and Distribution.

ISBN 978-1-55936-572-7 (paperback)
ISBN 978-1-55936-888-9 (ebook)

A catalog record for this book is available from the Library of Congress.

Book, cover design and composition by Lisa Govan

First Edition, September 2019

For T
Past, present, future

———ↄxxↄ———

with special thanks to Luke and Mindy
for all the conversations

Now I am ready to tell how bodies are changed
Into different bodies.

—OVID

She . . . changed from hour to hour, like mer-
cury. She was an odd bird; but she was a woman,
she wasn't a man, and I arrived at the conclusion
that a woman can change from one minute to the
next without anyone saying anything about it.

—PAUL BOWLES ON JANE BOWLES

A lot of people "love" because, and a lot of people "love" although, and a few individuals love.
Love is something illimitable and a lot of people
spend their limited lives trying to prevent anything illimitable from happening to them.

—E E CUMMINGS

Great sluts are made, not born.

—THE ETHICAL SLUT: A PRACTICAL GUIDE
TO POLYAMORY, OPEN RELATIONSHIPS
& OTHER ADVENTURES BY DOSSIE EASTON
AND JANET W. HARDY

How to transcend
a happy marriage

Production History

How to transcend a happy marriage had its world premiere at Lincoln Center Theater (André Bishop, Producing Artistic Director; Adam Siegel, Managing Director) in New York on March 20, 2017. It was directed by Rebecca Taichman. The scenic design was by David Zinn, the costume design was by Susan Hilferty, the lighting design was by Peter Kaczorowski, the sound design was by Matt Hubbs; the original music was by Todd Almond and the stage manager was Charles M. Turner III. The cast was:

GEORGE	Marisa Tomei
PAUL	Omar Metwally
JANE	Robin Weigert
MICHAEL	Brian Hutchison
PIP	Lena Hall
DAVID	Austin Smith
FREDDIE	David McElwee
JENNA	Naian González Norvind

PEOPLE

GEORGE (Georgia): In her late forties or so. Searching.

PAUL (married to George): In his late forties or so. Virile.

JANE: In her late forties or so. Capable.

MICHAEL (married to Jane): In his late forties or so. Sensitive.

PIP: A beautiful woman in her late twenties, named Deborah. Known to all as Pip. (She can dance and sing and slaughter animals.)

DAVID (pronounced Dah-veed): In a relationship with Pip and Freddie. A mathematician. He has a vaguely Slavic accent that is hard to place.

FREDDIE: Late twenties or early thirties. Gentle. And attractive to both sexes.

JENNA: A sixteen-year-old girl. Fierce, young, and tender. Michael and Jane's daughter.

Race and ethnicity are immaterial. Except that David is not from America.

WORLD

A forest.
A living/dining room.
A jail—empty space with a few bars.

A NOTE ON THE BIRD

At Lincoln Center, we used an actual bird, a dove, that appeared as if by magic in the penultimate scene. I cannot reveal how this bird appeared because a magician helped us make the bird appear, and I would not reveal his secrets. But equally acceptable are invisible birds that only the actors can see, toy birds, birds made of light and shadow, and puppet birds.

Prologue

The forest.
Forest sounds.
Steam rises from a recently slaughtered animal.
A woman—Pip—runs in toward the animal, which she has just killed.
She puts her arms around the animal.

If you cannot achieve this beautifully, go straight to Scene 1.

Act One

SCENE I

A domestic space.

A dinner table. Two women and two men eating dinner.
Some meat still on the table, and some nice vegetables.

JANE

So this woman at my office, a temp, she's incredibly beautiful, and very, you know *energetic*, and yesterday she came in with circles under her eyes and I said what's wrong are you tired? Yes, she said. Yes, I am. And I thought no wonder, because she's in this polyamorous relationship with two men—

GEORGE

What? Really?

JANE

Yes—

PAUL

They live together?

JANE

Yes.

GEORGE

Are the two men bi—or gay—or—

JANE

I'm not really sure but no I don't think so I think she's the hub—

MICHAEL

The *hub*?

JANE

Like, they have sex with her, the hub—but they don't necessarily all have sex with each other—

PAUL

Why not?

JANE

I haven't asked. But *anyway* so she came into work the other day tired—

GEORGE

I can imagine—I'd be so tired—

JANE

But not, as I'd suspected, from having sex with two men all weekend, but because she'd slaughtered a goat.

PAUL

A goat?

JANE

A goat. She slaughters all her own meat for the winter. She used to be a vegetarian but now she ethically slaughters her own meat—looks into its big brown soulful eyes, asks for forgiveness and then—

She makes a slicing motion.

GEORGE

Wow.

PAUL

Wow.

GEORGE

Why?

JANE

It's the idea that if you are willing to eat meat you should be willing to kill it. And eat all the parts of the animal in a respectful way.

GEORGE

I don't know if I could do that. Slaughter my own meat. Do you think I shouldn't eat meat if I can't bring myself to slaughter it?

PAUL

No. You don't walk around naked just because you don't know how to knit. You let someone else knit. Or sew. Or make your cheese.

GEORGE

Yes but I don't have an ethical revulsion towards knitting, or making cheese. I just don't know *how* to knit or make cheese—or I don't have *time* to do it—but I wouldn't *object* to doing it—

MICHAEL

So you'd have an ethical revulsion to slaughtering a goat, not just sort of distaste and lack of expertise?

GEORGE

Yes, right. I'd find it revolting. Like why my life for this goat's? The blood, the bones, the organs. I don't like eating meat that reminds me of flesh—ribs—drumsticks. I like sausage because it's barely meat anymore.

Do you think all world religions had at their heart animal sacrifice because we feel so intrinsically guilty about killing animals? So we made all these rules like kosher and—halal—and then Jesus came along and said don't worry about how you kill the meat, I'll die instead, and now we eat meat with impunity, but wasn't Jesus actually a vegetarian?

MICHAEL

I bet he was. Loaves of bread—fish—maybe a pescatarian he was—

JANE

Or a flexitarian—

PAUL

Either way, not all world religions started over guilt from animal sacrifice—that's just—well it's just basically false.

GEORGE

How do you know?

PAUL

There were rules for the meat, but that wasn't the reason for the religion—the guilt over animal killing—we're omnivores—

MICHAEL

But why do most spiritual practices think vegetarianism is a precondition for any spiritual progress?

PAUL

Even the Dalai Lama eats meat every other day. For his health, he says.

GEORGE

How would you know?

MICHAEL

But what I want to get back to is this: How does that woman have energy to have sex with two men then slaughter a goat?

PAUL

Maybe it *gives* her energy to have sex with two men. You're assuming she's like—drained—but maybe they're just pleasuring her constantly?

MICHAEL

Like tantric sex? Like the men never come they just make her orgasm over and over again?

JANE

Anyway, she says it's physically exhausting, killing *the goat*, all the physical labor, and it emotionally drains her as well. But it provides her with meat all winter.

GEORGE

Like sex with two men.

MICHAEL

So they live together?

JANE

Yes and it's tricky because it's hard to be *out* if you're polyamorous, people judge you, even, probably, you know, like in Portland.

GEORGE

Do they have sex all at the same time? Or one, and then the other?

JANE

I've never asked her. We're not that close.

PAUL

Why live together if you don't have sex all together?

GEORGE

There are other things to do when you live together besides have sex all the time. There are other household pleasures—or duties—they might share. Laundry, for example.

PAUL

Really polyamory takes all the fun out of adultery.

GEORGE

How do you mean?

PAUL

The lying the sneaking the will she or won't he—

GEORGE

Are you trying to tell me something?

PAUL

No, I'm just saying, the fun of adultery *in the abstract* seems to be partly the erotic tension around the secret, not the endless talking about—

GEORGE

Maybe you replace the pleasures of the secret with the pleasures of voyeurism.

PAUL

Are you trying to tell me something, George?

GEORGE

What do you think?

PAUL

So if you wanted to add a third—would you go for a two women hub situation or two men—

GEORGE

Two women—

MICHAEL

Two women definitely—

JANE

Me too.

PAUL

Really? With two women—all the talking about it—the emotional processing—

GEORGE

That's true. It would be exhausting. All the talking.

JANE

But two men—all of the laundry—

GEORGE

But if they did the laundry themselves and spent most of the time in the boudoir competing to pleasure you—

15

JANE

That's true.

PAUL

I imagine women would have an easier time sharing a man than two men sharing—

JANE

Why?

PAUL

Because most men are so insecure about, you know, size.

JANE

What? That's ridiculous. Women don't even care about size.

PAUL   MICHAEL

Don't they?   Really?

JANE AND GEORGE

No!

JANE

I mean, if you go online and look up: "I'm worried that my husband's penis is too dot dot dot"—it comes out automatically as big. Women are worried it's too big and they'll get *harmed* by it.

MICHAEL

Have you been looking online typing: "I'm worried my husband's penis is too big"?

JANE

No, sorry.

MICHAEL

Oh—I was preparing to be flattered.

GEORGE

I once had an Italian boyfriend who was so large it *worried me*. I was a virgin, I thought he would gore me, impale me—

JANE

Pass the asparagus.

PAUL

So did you take pity on her—the polyamorous temp—and I don't know, give her the day off after she slaughtered the goat?

JANE

She's not the sort of person you pity. As I said, she's very energetic.

GEORGE

Is she beautiful? I like to think that she's beautiful.

JANE

She is.

PAUL

What does she look like?

JANE

Do you want to see her picture?

Taking out her phone.

PAUL

No! I don't want to see her picture. I want to imagine her. Does she have long hair or short?

JANE

(Indicating the length of the actress's hair) Sort of like this.

17

GEORGE

Oh! What does she wear?

JANE

She wears culottes a lot.

MICHAEL

Culottes a lot?

GEORGE

(Overlapping) The shorts—

PAUL

Does she move like a panther or a cat or a bull or a snake?

JANE

Panther.

MICHAEL

I knew it!

JANE

I was just kidding. She's a *temp*. She moves like a temp. A temp at a legal aid office with a lot of—physical energy.

They murmur.

JANE

Are you all imagining having sex with her right now?

MICHAEL, GEORGE, AND PAUL

(A chorus, variations of) Yes, yeah, uh-huh.

JANE

Hmm.

PAUL

(To Michael) Have you met her?

MICHAEL

No. I haven't met her. Have I?

GEORGE

You'd remember if you'd met her.

JANE

She's more ordinary than you might think. You're getting all caught up.

PAUL

There is no way this woman is ordinary. This goat-slaughtering, culotte-wearing woman. I bet she wears the dead fur of animals into an airport, smelling feral, slightly of fur—

MICHAEL

—and patchouli and a little metallic smell of blood.

PAUL

She doesn't shave. The way she holds her feet when she stands, slightly imbalanced—

MICHAEL

—with generous thighs—

GEORGE

Enough!

JANE

I could invite her over for dinner.

GEORGE

Would it be rude to invite her and not invite the men-folk—her what do you call it—partners? Husbands?

JANE

I don't think they're married.

MICHAEL

Let's invite them all over!

GEORGE

But what would you cook? Would she bring the carcass and you make a big goat stew for seven?

MICHAEL

Why can't she settle down with one man I wonder?

GEORGE

Let's ask her at dinner!

JANE

I think that might be rude. I think in the polyamory movement, you sort of just—accept—the person's sexual predilections.

PAUL

Is it a movement now?

MICHAEL

I think so. There's a book—called *The Ethical Slut*. It tells you how to do it.

JANE

Why were you reading *The Ethical Slut*?

GEORGE	MICHAEL
That's not a title, is it?	I—

MICHAEL

It is a title.

PAUL

A title does not a movement make.

GEORGE

What's the difference between a movement and a fad?

PAUL

Movements involve oppression; fads involve predilection.

GEORGE

So you're saying it's a fad?

JANE

I think polyamorous people are discriminated against. Like—there's no box to check at the doctor's office—single, married, widowed—poly—I think it's next now after gay marriage—

PAUL

But it's not a continuum—like gay, polyamorous—they're different lines—

GEORGE

But it's a civil rights issue, isn't it?

PAUL

Let's invite this temp over for supper. I'll slaughter some meat.

GEORGE

If she comes will you seriously slaughter an animal?

PAUL

Sure. I once slaughtered a rooster in Morocco.

GEORGE

You did? Why didn't you tell me?

PAUL

It never came up. It was before your time.

GEORGE

Oh.

MICHAEL

What was it like? Killing the rooster.

PAUL

Sort of awful. You could tell the rooster didn't want to die, it didn't want to come with me. And I slit its throat and put it in a hamper and its body was still going even after the neck was slit and it jerked around in this hamper—

MICHAEL

Did you like eating it? Did it add to your pleasure or detract from your pleasure that you killed the rooster yourself?

PAUL

Added to it. Definitely.

JANE

Wow. Do you think that's a gender thing? Like, it might add to my pleasure eating a cucumber or a lettuce leaf knowing I'd grown it in the ground myself, knowing I'd helped nurture something into existence, but I don't think it would add to my pleasure eating a rooster after I'd slit its throat.

PAUL

(To Jane) Well your temp is a woman and she likes killing her own animals.

JANE

For ethical reasons, not for bloodlust.

GEORGE

What's her name anyway?

JANE

What do you imagine her name is?

GEORGE

Greta.

PAUL

Miranda.

JANE

Well it's Deborah.

GEORGE

No! Such bad nicknames for Deborah. Debbie. No wonder she can't be satisfied with one man—

PAUL

You're so judgmental.

GEORGE

About her name?

PAUL

No. About assuming that the goal is to be monogamous.

JANE

Actually all her friends call her Pip.

GEORGE

Pip?

PAUL

My name is Deborah but my friends call me *Pip*? Like where do you get Pip from Deborah?

JANE

I have no idea.

GEORGE

Now who's judgmental.

PAUL

You're assuming that she's damaged or defective in some way because she isn't a prairie vole.

JANE

What?

PAUL

Prairie voles are intrinsically monogamous and sort of huddle together all their lives and non-prairie voles huddle with multiple partners.

MICHAEL

Oh right I read about that in the *Atlantic*, I think.

PAUL

So let's look at our calendars. When can we invite Deborah and the gentlemen over? I'll slaughter a duck for dinner. A duck seems a good start. You have more sympathy for mammals, right? Better to start with fowl?

JANE

What about the fourth of December?

PAUL

I can't do the fourth—I have that talk.

GEORGE

What talk?

PAUL

Post-colonial Dutch architecture.

GEORGE

Right.

JANE

The seventh?

GEORGE

That's Daphne's nutcracker recital.

JANE

Seventeenth—no . . . hmm . . .

PAUL

Eighteenth?

GEORGE

Theo's first violin recital!

PAUL

Oh right.

JANE

Is Theo taking violin now too?

GEORGE

Yes!

JANE

Oh! So now all of them could form a little trio—

PAUL

The twentieth?

MICHAEL

We leave for Hawaii on the twentieth.

GEORGE

I'm so jealous.

JANE

This will have to wait for the New Year.

GEORGE

What about New Year's Eve? Are you back for New Year's Eve?

JANE

Yes!

PAUL

That would be a nice way to ring in the new year. Deborah and a slaughtered duck.

GEORGE

Could we really get a sitter for New Year's? It's the worst night of the year to get a sitter.

MICHAEL

Well you wouldn't really need a sitter you could bring the kids and they could play video games upstairs?

GEORGE

No, let's get a sitter.

JANE

So New Year's Eve then.

PAUL

Till then.

ALL

Till then!

Scene 2

George and Paul turn toward the audience.
Perhaps they change an article of clothing or two, getting ready for
a party.

GEORGE
(To the audience) And our lives would change, forever.

PAUL
At first she seemed quite ordinary.

GEORGE
Pip.

PAUL
A young woman in her twenties.

28

GEORGE

As if that's in any way ordinary, from the point of view of a man in his forties.

PAUL

And her lovers—also ordinary—

GEORGE

But for the love they both had for this woman—
she was so beautiful she could make all her own rules—

PAUL

Was it her beauty or the capaciousness of her desire?

GEORGE

Or both?
At any rate—

PAUL

At any rate— *(Back to George)* Let's go—

GEORGE

Do you have enough cash to pay the sitter?

PAUL

Yes.

GEORGE

I'm worried.

PAUL

Why?

GEORGE

She's never put Daphne to sleep before and you know how Daphne can be—

PAUL

It'll be fine. Let's go.

George hesitates.

PAUL

What's wrong?

GEORGE

I'm scared.

PAUL

Of what?

GEORGE

What if we all get drunk and Deborah or Pip and her husbands bring that hallucinatory drug from the Amazon—I think it's called ayahuasca—

PAUL

You can buy hallucinogenic drugs now on Amazon?

GEORGE

No no from *The Amazon* and we ritually drink it and then she suggests we slaughter an animal and then we do and we slosh around in animal blood and then we wake up and it's our own children we've slaughtered?

PAUL

Have you been reading *The Bacchae* again?

GEORGE

You know I never managed to learn Greek. It's one of my embarrassments. Latin came so easily—

PAUL

You could read it in translation.

GEORGE

Yes, I could.

PAUL

You could order it from the Amazon.

GEORGE

Ha ha.

PAUL

Anyway. Our children will be home. With a babysitter.

GEORGE

A *new* babysitter—what do I even know about her—I didn't check her references—her smile is sort of vampiric—

PAUL

(Reassuring) It's just her lipstick, it's black—

GEORGE

Right, who wears black lipstick?

PAUL

She goes to *Barnard*—

GEORGE

I don't know even why we're going out—we should stay in and do our Christmas cards which are late—again—they'll be New Year's cards—

PAUL

It was you who wanted to meet her. Pip.

31

GEORGE

I thought it was you.

A moment.

PAUL

At any rate they're expecting us and we'll all just play Scrabble like we always do and fall asleep before the New Year.

GEORGE

Do you have the duck?

PAUL

Yes.

GEORGE

Fine. Let's go.

PAUL

Don't linger.

GEORGE

What?

PAUL

Don't linger. Saying good night to the children. It only makes the leaving worse.

Scene 3

New Year's Eve at Jane and Michael's house.
Festive hats on the table.
Pip is beautiful.
But more ordinary than you might think.
In fact, it might be her ordinary relationship with
her fearless sensuality which does not require deodorant or lipstick
that makes everyone immediately think about sex.
She is unvarnished and unashamed.

PAUL
(To Pip) Nice to meet you. I'm sorry about the duck.

PIP
What?

PAUL
I tried to kill one, I really did—

The below section overlaps.

GEORGE

He did kill it actually—

PAUL

I did kill it—

GEORGE

And then we cooked it

PAUL

and it tasted

GEORGE

terrible

PAUL

really

GEORGE

sinewy

PAUL

fowl

GEORGE

ducky

PAUL

the smell of dead feathers

GEORGE

which I tried to cover with paprika

34

PAUL

and garlic

GEORGE

but it was no use—

PAUL

we worried we'd make everyone *sick*

GEORGE

like happy new year, happy avian bird flu—
we thought we would kill everyone by accident so:

PAUL

Peking duck from Han's!

JANE

Great!

MICHAEL

I love Peking duck.

PIP

You slaughtered a duck for us? For me?

PAUL

Well we heard you didn't eat meat that wasn't specially killed for
you.

PIP

Oh!

GEORGE

I mean Jane said you wanted to be sure it was ethically slaughtered, that you knew where it came from, how it got to be dead—

PIP

That's so *thoughtful.* No one's ever done that for me, at a dinner party before—

PAUL

Do you usually bring your own meat, like BYOM?

PIP

I usually just eat vegetables. Unless I know how the animal was—you know—slaughtered.

JANE

What did you do with the dead duck? The one with paprika?

GEORGE

It's in the garbage.

PIP

(Horrified) Oh!!!

FREDDIE

(Sadly) Oh.

GEORGE

I suppose that's even worse—wasting it—oh dear—

PIP

It's okay—

DAVID

How did it feel, to kill the duck?

PAUL

Well—it was alive and then it was dead.

GEORGE

I wanted to say some kind of prayer over it like some kosher butcher prayer but I didn't know any and that made me sad. Then I cleaned the blood up. And I didn't want to use our hand towels to clean up the blood but it took two rolls of paper towels—recycled—to clean up all the blood.

PAUL

(To Pip) Anyway, can you eat this duck? If you didn't kill it yourself?

GEORGE

As the Chinese restaurant didn't kill this duck particularly for you—

PAUL

Though I'm sure they would have if—

PIP

If—

PAUL

If they'd met you. They would have killed for you.

PIP

Is that a compliment?

GEORGE

It's a compliment, disguised as a comment.

A moment.

MICHAEL

Champagne?

GEORGE AND PAUL

Sure! Yes!

FREDDIE

Oh, and we brought dessert. Hash brownies. They're vegan. A humble offering. For those who don't drink.

JANE

Oh, thanks.

GEORGE

Thanks.

A pause. They settle in with their drinks.

GEORGE

So—do you all hunt together?

DAVID

No, only Pip hunts.

FREDDIE

When she killed her first deer David and I were eating pizza at Dellarocco's.

They laugh, remembering. They all have a glass of champagne.

FREDDIE

I'm a vegan.

GEORGE

Oh?

DAVID

And I don't eat shrimps.

MICHAEL

Do you have an allergy?

DAVID

Not really they just seem pitiful. So—small.

GEORGE

I don't like shrimp either.

DAVID

Is that a kosher thing?

GEORGE

No, it's just—sad story. Forget it.

DAVID

Tell.

GEORGE

Well when I was eighteen I was sent on a mission to get fried shrimp for my father who had cancer. I went all the way to the fish market to get the fried shrimp, it was all he asked for from his yellow sick bed, in this small voice. I thought he might throw it up, I thought it might be bad for his stomach with the chemotherapy and all, so I bought healthy bland fish and rice. How dare I, with my misplaced teenage pieties about health. Anyway I came back with two plates of fish and he looked at me with watery eyes and said where is the fried shrimp? I'll go back for you, I'll get it, I said. And I did. He died the following week.

DAVID

Oh. I'm sorry.

JANE

That is so sad, George.

PAUL

Sorry, honey. You never told me that. God.

GEORGE

Well, it's no big deal. I'm just not fond of shrimp. Sorry. Anyway.

DAVID

Please—don't apologize for your loss. You are too beautiful to do something so American.

Small awkward pause.

JANE

So, Dah-veed, where are you from?

DAVID

Are you having trouble placing my accent?

JANE

Oh no it's just—

DAVID

I'm from everywhere. And nowhere. I moved constantly as a child—Egypt, Israel, Ghana, Bulgaria, Pittsburgh—as a result, I don't really believe in nationality.

JANE	GEORGE
Oh!	Mm.

MICHAEL

Should we eat?

JANE

It's only six o'clock. Maybe crudités?

MICHAEL

Crudités! I'll get them.

Michael exits.

JANE

So—Pip—do you hunt by yourself or with a group?

PIP

Well I don't hunt—the goats—obviously. I go to a sustainable
farm upstate and pick one out and kill it.

JANE

(Polite interest) Oh.

PIP

And in Brooklyn I butcher pigs. But when I hunt deer—yes, I go
with a group.

GEORGE

Where?

PIP

New Jersey. Usually.

DAVID

Plentiful deer in New Jersey. They've become a nuisance really.
Like squirrels.

JANE

And why did you start killing your own animals?

PIP

Well I used to be a vegetarian but then I found I didn't have much
energy and it turned out my iron was low? And then coinciden-
tally I went to Africa. And I saw the Masai slaughter—or sac-

rifice—a goat which they do every one to two days and it was really *amazing*. They would bind the goat's legs and then suffocate it with their hands and then a child—it was a great honor to be this child—would drink some of the goat's blood—and then they would cook and eat or use every part of the animal I mean *every part*—they actually repurposed the asshole and made it into a ring.

Pip shows Jane the ring.

JANE

Oh!

PIP

And I thought—Jesus Christ we in the West are so *wasteful*.

GEORGE   JANE
Mm.   Oh.

PIP

So I thought, when I come back to the States, if I do eat an animal to get my iron count up, I will kill it myself, and use every part of it.

PAUL

And is your iron up?

PIP

Oh yes! I have so much more energy.

PAUL

You seem energetic.

DAVID

She is.

They all drink.

GEORGE

So, David, what do you do?

JANE

Dah-veed—

GEORGE

Dah-veed—

DAVID

I do differential geometry.

PIP

He studies triangles and things.

PAUL

(Laughing) Really?

DAVID

You find differential geometry funny?

PAUL

No it's just um—triangles.

DAVID

(Not laughing) Oh. Right.

PAUL

Sorry that was dumb.

GEORGE

Yup.

PAUL

Differential geometry you were saying?

DAVID

Well I was studying the relationship between Wittgenstein's philosophy of mathematics and the views of his teacher Bertrand Russell and then I thought this is too language-based I'll go back to basics, to Pythagoras. No one has done any decent work on triangles in a very long time. A triangle, I think, is a propitiator of magic. Jokes come in three, so does the Godhead. People ask me: isn't two enough? Why add a third? But no one asks the Holy Trinity—isn't two enough? Why add a third?

Polite murmurs from the group.

DAVID

People say: a perfect triangle. But they don't say a perfect square. Why do we call boring people square? A square is two couples playing bridge.
A triangle is the strongest shape. Not a square. Not a line.

PAUL

Yes! When you make a geodesic dome you fold triangles together and you get the strongest structure in the world.

DAVID

Yes.

GEORGE

Paul is an architect.

PAUL

Well sort of.

DAVID

How can you sort of be an architect?

GEORGE

He's still technically an architect but after a while he stopped building things and started making up theories about architecture and writing books about his theories.

DAVID

What kind of theories?

PAUL

Oh, mostly about ideas of home—like why do we still all crowd around in the kitchen even when there is no fire or hearth there anymore?

FREDDIE

Huh.

GEORGE

He's actually sort of famous. Among architects.

DAVID

I guess the most famous architects don't build anything anymore.

PAUL

I couldn't do one more fucking bathroom renovation. No matter how lucrative.

GEORGE

Funnily enough writing about the idea of architecture isn't very lucrative. That's why I gave up pursuing my PhD in classics and started teaching junior high Latin. To pay for our children's education, which we otherwise couldn't afford.

PAUL

George wants me to go back to doing bathroom renovations.

GEORGE

There are other things in houses—in *homes*—besides bathrooms.

An awkward pause.
She drinks.

FREDDIE

I love Latin. It's such a beautiful language. I think its beauty is why it died. It's too beautiful for this world. Like so many things.

GEORGE

Thank you. I mean, why am I saying thank you, I didn't invent Latin.

FREDDIE

Maybe because you were embarrassed that you revealed too much to strangers and then I changed the subject.

GEORGE

Yes. Thank you for that. You're so lovely, you really are.

Michael comes back with crudités.

MICHAEL

Olives? Nuts?

JANE

Dah-veed is a mathematician. He studies Pythagoras.

MICHAEL

Really?

DAVID

Yes.

JANE

My husband is interested in math. He's very good at math.

MICHAEL

Not like you are. More like. Well. I got interested when I was study-ing music theory.

DAVID

You are a musician?

JANE

He is.

All murmur.

MICHAEL

I write jingles. I used to be in a rock band but we toured too much, so when we had a kid I started to write jingles.

JANE

Have you ever heard: *Don't you dare buy just ONE buy ten of them, buy ten!*
That's Michael's. Have you heard it?

FREDDIE

We don't have a TV.

JANE

Oh.

DAVID

But you are interested in mathematics?

MICHAEL

Well I'm interested in how Pythagoras said "All is number" and how he thought everything in the world could be described by numbers but now we live in this hyper-numerical world, and we willfully submit to big data and Amazon's predictions of what books and products we might like— But it's a sort of perversion of what Pythagoras had in mind—

PAUL

Which was—

MICHAEL

A more spiritual idea of numbers.

PAUL   DAVID

Such as—   Exactly!

MICHAEL

Well number 1 is the number of reason,
2 is the number of opinion,
3 is the number of harmony.

DAVID

(Overlapping) —harmony. I'm amazed you know all this; usually
you tell someone you're studying Pythagoras and they say oh yes
triangles, two short sides, one long side—

MICHAEL

Yes, the shortcut!

DAVID

And I nod my head oh yes yes the Pythagorean theorem.

MICHAEL

Yes! And really he invented harmony, like can you imagine, being
the guy who discovered harmony? Who discovered triads and
the circle of fifths?

GEORGE

I get so excited when people talk about music theory or any other
language I don't understand.

PAUL

(To George) Octave—

MICHAEL

(To George) Fifth—

PAUL

(To George, seductive) Pamplemousse.

GEORGE

Oh!

PIP

Really? Not me. My brain shuts off when people talk about numbers. Let's not talk about math. Let's do something.

MICHAEL

We could read *Twelfth Night* out loud.

JANE

He likes to start each New Year reading a play out loud. We have a little reading club.

DAVID

Oh, that's cute.

MICHAEL

Shakespeare wrote it for twelve days after Christmas for the queen, it's almost twelve days after Christmas now, isn't it?

DAVID

Six.

PAUL

That's right, you're the mathematician.

DAVID

And architects are notoriously bad at math—

PAUL

That's true.

MICHAEL

The soul of our grandam might haply inhabit a bird
What thinkst thou of his opinion?
I think nobly of the soul, and no way approve of his opinion.
Fare thee well. Remain thou still in darkness: thou shalt hold
the opinion of Pythagoras ere I will allow of thy wits; and
fear to kill a woodcock, lest thou dispossess the soul of thy
grandma.

They all applaud.

JANE

Wow!

DAVID

Brava!

PAUL

Well done!

MICHAEL

I played Malvolio. In college.

GEORGE

You're full of surprises tonight!

PAUL

So you can play Malvolio!

GEORGE

I call Olivia! Is that her name, the one who disguises herself as a
boy or is that the other one, the sad one?

DAVID

I'm not much of an actor.

PIP

(Pronouncing "karaoke" with Japanese pronunciation) Do you have karaoke?

JANE

What? Oh, karaoke? I think Jenna used to have a karaoke machine— is it in the basement? She's outgrown it—

PIP

I LOVE karaoke.

JANE

Okay, let me see if I can find it down there—I'll be back!

Jane leaves.

FREDDIE

Brownie?

PAUL

Sure.

Paul eats one.

GEORGE

They look delicious, gooey and still warm. But do you think it will be out of my system tomorrow? We are hosting a potluck.

FREDDIE

Oh definitely.

GEORGE

All right, I'll try. You?

She eats a brownie. They pass the brownies and eat them.

FREDDIE

I'm driving. No thanks.

GEORGE

Oh.

PAUL

So what sort of thing do you like to sing?

PIP

Oh—anything—

FREDDIE

She's a really good singer.

MICHAEL

Yeah?

PIP

It used to be my thing. Singing—well, and acting—I gave it up.

GEORGE

Why'd you give it up?

PIP

I wanted to help the world. That's why I became a temp. "Ha ha."

PAUL

Surely you won't be a temp forever surely it's *temporary*. Ha ha.

PIP

Yes I hope so I'm in massage school. But I don't want to work in spas. I want to be a body worker.

GEORGE

I used to think body work was the stupidest word, but then I went to California—and this body worker pressed on a little point above my heart until I cried and I realized there really is a difference between a body worker and a massage therapist.

PIP

Yes. There is. I want to give massages to the terminally ill to help them die.

MICHAEL

That's really good of you.

PIP

Thank you.

DAVID

She's got really strong hands.

PAUL

I bet.

PIP

Anyway, now I just sing in the shower.

PAUL

You guys must have a big shower—

FREDDIE

Not really. Regular sized.

PAUL

Do you shower all together—or—

PIP

Do *you?*

GEORGE

Sometimes. For special occasions.

PAUL

Do you have a really big bed? Like a California king?

PIP

How do you know we don't all have separate beds? Or sleep on the floor?

PAUL

Do you?

PIP

I'm not telling. You seem awfully curious though.

GEORGE

That's my husband. Curious George!

DAVID

(To George) I thought *your* name was George.

GEORGE

Yes it is, short for Georgia.

DAVID

Oh. A girl called George—that's sexy.

GEORGE

You wouldn't think so if you lived in Australia. My mother is Australian. A lot of girls are called George there.

DAVID

I'd find it even more sexy. I like the accent too.

George blushes.

GEORGE

So are you all, like, *married?*

Pip, David, and Freddie look at each other.

PIP

No . . . we're thinking about it.
For a while I never believed in marriage because you know, the patriarchy . . .

George and Paul and Michael murmur with understanding.

PIP

But if we do have kids we would have a ceremony and close the threesome to outsiders.
For now, we have sort of, rules, about play.

GEORGE   PAUL
Ah.   Oh.

GEORGE

Like what sorts of rules?
I'm sorry, I'm prying. It's none of my business.

PIP

Life is boring without prying.

FREDDIE

Our main rule is radical honesty.

David and George murmur in agreement.

PIP

And if we sleep with anyone else we have to introduce them to the group. And close friends are off limits. And that's basically it. We don't like having too many rules.

DAVID

We find it baroque.

PAUL

Right. So how do you introduce each other—like these are my partners?

PIP

Someone invented the word throuple but it's sort of a horrible word isn't it?

DAVID

Our language is limited and so our imagination is limited.

GEORGE

I agree!

PAUL

Unless it's the other way around.

GEORGE

Have you always been in—throuples?

DAVID

I prefer the word triad.

GEORGE

Triads, then?

PIP

(Gesturing to the couples) I remember when I was a child and imagined growing up and being married to one man, all alone in a house together, it just seemed so *lonely* to me. So exposed, so small. No—camaraderie.

Sometimes I think I'm a gay man trapped in a woman's body. But then I think, no, I like my breasts and I really like to have sex with women too. So . . .

A moment.

MICHAEL

Olives anyone?

FREDDIE

Sometimes I find it embarrassing saying: I'm bisexual. It's like, aren't we all?
It's like declaring—I'm coming out as human, everyone.

DAVID

Being human is an embarrassment.

PIP

The thing about being bisexual that's tedious is you constantly have to announce yourself. It's like, but if you decide to be a vegetarian, you don't go around reminding people, well I'm technically an omnivore. You know?

PAUL

So if you're a monogamous bisexual, does that make you a liar all the time?

DAVID

I sort of think so. But monogamy is a construct that will seem passé in the next century. So will race. The whole world will be like Brazil.

GEORGE

I love Brazil.

MICHAEL

Pistachios?

FREDDIE

Yes, please. I love pistachios at a party. Gives you something to do with your hands. I never know what to do with my hands while I make small talk.

GEORGE

Me too.

FREDDIE

Here, pistachio.

He opens one for her.

GEORGE

Oh. Thank you. Although opening it for me sort of defeats the purpose, doesn't it? Of allaying anxiety while making small talk?

FREDDIE

Yes. I think I might like opening them as much as I like eating them. And I like the salt.

MICHAEL

Mm, me too. Unsalted pistachios are bunk. But inside the dark and salt of them, and the sound they make when you finally get inside one.

GEORGE   PIP

Uh-huh.   Mmm.

MICHAEL

You know those impenetrable pistachios, the ones you finally
have to discard?

FREDDIE

I hate throwing anything away. I would not throw away an uneaten
pistachio.

GEORGE

(To Freddie) What do you do anyway?

FREDDIE

Nothing really.

GEORGE

I mean for a job.

FREDDIE

Yeah, I try not to do anything. It's kind of a philosophy. I think,
I walk. I try not to leave any imprint. Or footprint. I don't buy
anything. I collect garbage and make it into things. And I grow
vegetables in the garden. And take care of household things.

GEORGE

Oh.

FREDDIE

I went to Harvard.

GEORGE

Oh!

FREDDIE

That's neither here nor there I don't know why I said that.

GEORGE

No, I can see that.

FREDDIE

That I went to Harvard?

GEORGE

Sure, I can see doing nothing afterwards. Nothing can compare, right?

FREDDIE

It's not that—it's more of a choice.

MICHAEL

(To Freddie) How did you and Pip meet?

FREDDIE

I was taking a discarded garbage can out of her garbage bin.

PAUL

She was throwing a garbage in a garbage?

FREDDIE

Yes. And I didn't have a garbage, because I don't throw anything away. So I reclaimed it. As a planter? And we became friends. And we became a little household.

GEORGE

It's like our whole culture.

FREDDIE

What?

GEORGE

A garbage in a garbage.

They all murmur in agreement.

PIP

(About her pistachio which she can't open) This pistachio is impossible.

She hands it to Paul who opens it with his teeth.
He has an animal victory over the pistachio.

PAUL

Here is the truth about teeth. We are omnivores. Fucking omnivores. We have these fangs. These, my friend, were not made to chew on blades of grass, to munch on bunny food, they were meant to tear apart animal tissue.

GEORGE

I think you just opened a very small pistachio.

Jane comes back dragging a karaoke machine.

JANE

I finally found it! I've no idea what songs are on it. It might only have kids songs—"Let It Go"—

PIP

I *love* "Let It Go."

PAUL

Mmm.

JANE

So,
Who is first?

PIP

I'll go.

GEORGE

(To Jane) Brownie?

JANE

Maybe just a nibble.

PIP

(About the karaoke machine) How does this thing work?

MICHAEL

(Pressing buttons) Here—

PIP

(Scrolling through songs) Let's see . . . "If You're Happy and You
Know It"; "Part of Your World," *The Little Mermaid* . . .

GEORGE

(To David) What is it with mermaids? Would you want to have
sex with a mermaid?

DAVID

Sure I'd fuck a mermaid, absolutely.

MICHAEL

But where are their vaginas?

GEORGE

Their whole lower half is like one big vagina and all breasts on
top, it's the perfect male fantasy, they can't walk, no legs, so you
can fuck them and then throw them back into the water. They
can't run away.

PIP

There are so few advantages to being a mermaid.

DAVID

The whole ocean could be your bidet.

GEORGE

Does it have "Wild Thing"? That's the only song I know how to play on the guitar. "Wild thing . . . you make my heart sing . . . you make everything—groovy—da da da da DAH DAH"

PIP

(About the song) No they don't have it—

A fragment of an instrumental eighties song with a synthesizer.

GEORGE

Everything went downhill in the eighties. Synthesizers! And being so lonely you have to harmonize with yourself.

DAVID

I blame it all on Ronald Reagan, personally.

GEORGE

Me too!

PIP

Isn't it sad when a singer harmonizes with themselves? It's like: couldn't you have found *one other person* to harmonize with? And it's obvious they aren't singing in real time because they had to sing the harmony on top of the melody so it's like they took the music out of time?

GEORGE

Yes! And how fucking lonely, you know, to harmonize with yourself? I know, back-up singers are passé, but fuck.

PAUL

You're stoned, darling.

63

PIP

Okay, I think I found a good one.

Music comes on, a kid version of "She'll Be Comin' 'Round the Mountain."
They have all drunk some champagne by now,
eaten some pistachios and hash brownies. Except for Freddie, who is driving.
Pip sings; she's breathtaking and sexy it is almost too much to bear.
They are all driven wild with desire.

PIP

She'll be comin' 'round the mountain when she comes
She'll be comin' 'round the mountain when she comes
She'll be comin' 'round the mountain
She'll be comin' 'round the mountain
She'll be comin' 'round the mountain when she comes—

She'll be riding six white horses when she comes
She'll be riding six white horses when she comes
Yee-ha—

Hold on a second—

Pip adjusts the karaoke machine and a slow sensual beat comes on;
she sings on top of it.
The mood changes.

PIP

She'll be riding six white horses
She'll be riding six white horses
She'll be riding six white horses when she comes

PAUL

Yee-ha.

PIP

She'll be wearing red pajamas when she comes
(so soft!)
She'll be wearing red pajamas when she comes

JANE

So soft!

PIP

She'll be wearing red pajamas
She'll be wearing red pajamas
She'll be wearing red pajamas when she comes

She'll have to sleep with grandma when she comes—

MICHAEL

Are these really the words?

PIP

She'll have to sleep with grandma when she comes
Oh she'll have to sleep with someone
She'll have to sleep with someone
She'll have to sleep with someone when she comes

Oh we'll all go out to meet her when she comes

DAVID

Hi babe

PIP

Oh we'll all go out to meet her when she comes
We'll all go out to meet her
We'll all go out to meet her

MICHAEL

Jesus Christ.

PIP

We'll all go out to meet her when she comes

ALL

Hi babe, so soft, yee-ha!

A dance break in the music.

GEORGE

You're a good dancer.

PIP

I've been taking pole dancing classes. To work out. It's kind of liberating. Here let me show you. Do you have any poles here?

JANE   MICHAEL

No.   No—

Pip dances with Jane.

PIP

But if you imagine that *you're* the pole—

Jane moans.

JANE

Oh, excuse me.

PIP

We'll be singin' hallelujah when she comes

FREDDIE

Hallelujah

PIP

We'll be singin' hallelujah when she comes

GEORGE

Jesus how many times does she come?

PIP

We'll be singin' hallelujah
We'll be singin' hallelujah
We'll be singin' hallelujah when she comes!

JANE

Hallelujah

MICHAEL

I've heard that song before but I feel like I've never heard that song before.

PAUL

You're a really good singer.

PIP

Thank you.

DAVID

(To Jane and Michael) So where's your daughter anyway?

JANE

She's at a friend's house.

MICHAEL

Her friend will drive her home at 12:30 or she'll give us a call.

JANE

She won't call. Life with a teenager is a series of reprimands until your personality disappears.

MICHAEL

You're stoned, Jane. In any case, she's sixteen, so she only has a learner's permit.

PIP

So we can play until 12:30!

DAVID

Great!

FREDDIE

Great.

PAUL

Great.

PIP

And then we all turn into pumpkins!

They laugh wildly as though Pip said something very funny.

GEORGE

Wait, is it the New Year? Is it midnight already? I thought I heard the neighbors banging pots and pans!

JANE

Is it midnight? Where are the clocks? Who has a phone?

PIP

I once heard that whatever you're doing on New Year's Eve at midnight you'll be doing spiritually for the whole year!

FREDDIE

Yes, it's midnight!

They blow on noisemakers.

ALL

Happy New Year!

The couples all kiss each other. Then people start kissing in general.

ALL

Happy New Year, Happy New Year!

During the following, we see the orgy through her language rather than through their bodies.

GEORGE

(To the audience) And what began with New Year's kisses became, well suddenly it was this incredibly pornographic scene, like penises everywhere, so many of them, and sprouting tendrils of hair, sort of blossoming out between hands, lips everywhere, this strange jungle garden just sprouting out in the living room, like in *Where the Wild Things Are*—
"And in his bedroom a forest grew, and the walls became the world all around"—

ALL

"LET THE WILD RUMPUS BEGIN!"

A forest appears on the walls, the living room dragged away.

GEORGE

And you know how in *Where the Wild Things Are*, when the wild rumpus begins, there are no words for three pages, just pictures of hairy monsters riding on monsters and jungle overhang and climbing vines and that's how it was—the words poured out into silence and there was no sound just people riding each other and suddenly there were so many bodies, up against this blue paisley living room furniture and the tasteful throws were stained with fluids—and it was carnal and it was—there were so many open-ings and closings and every which way—and I was—I don't even want to tell you what I was doing—someone was tasting me, someone else was making me taste myself, and it was dirty but I felt sort of gloriously clean.

And time slowed down. And I just started to notice that some people had thick fingers inside me and some people had slender fingers and I was thinking do I like the thick fingers or the slender ones better, the skin that's soft and oily or the dry rough skin against my cheek—and I looked over at my husband and he was kissing my best friend and something in his eyes terrified me—and then there was this little sound, this little scuffle, like a bunny rabbit caught in the bushes—a squeak in the hinges, and a door opened, and in walks Jane and Michael's teenage daughter, my goddaughter in fact.

And we all turned towards her.

And Jane said in this very maternal voice:

JANE
Jenna, what happened, I was going to pick you up.

GEORGE
And Jane had a rather enormous penis in her hand which then limply slid behind a geranium and her daughter Jenna said:

JENNA
Yeah, well, that party was kind of lame, there was drinking and I *don't like to drink*—so I came home. What the FUCK? And you know what else? You're all fat. Your flesh has gravity. It's embarrassing. What do you think you are, like twenty-two? Jesus!

GEORGE
And then she turned around and went out the door. We looked down at our bodies and we were ashamed.

They all look down at their bodies, ashamed. They look up.

70

GEORGE

And it was not the adults who took the children out of the garden but the children who forced the adults out of the garden.

And I thought: Oh—it's all because we killed that duck. We slaughtered a duck and didn't eat it. And that must be very, very bad luck.

Blackout.

Act Two

SCENE I

The forest.
George and Pip sitting with hunting gear.
Orange hunting pinnies over their clothes.
A large silver bow and arrow.
For a moment they wait; watching and eating trail mix.
It's cold out, early January in the wilds of New Jersey.

A rustling.
George jumps.

GEORGE

A deer—

PIP

No—that was a bird—see? In the branches? It's flown away.

GEORGE

Oh!

PIP

Are you okay? You seem jumpy.

GEORGE

I've never been hunting before. Archery at summer camp, but no live target.

PIP

Right.

GEORGE

Thanks for taking me. I haven't been myself since New Year's Eve. Since my goddaughter ran away.

PIP

Your goddaughter ran away?

GEORGE

Jenna. Jane's daughter? I'm her godmother.

PIP

Oh. So you're responsible for her spiritual education?

GEORGE

Not really.

PIP

So in what way are you—

GEORGE

Uh—in the way that people are godparents now, like they're close friends of the parents and make an extra effort to remember their birthday and give them presents—

PIP

So it's not really religious—you're—just like an official friend of
the family?

GEORGE

Yes. I'm an official—anyway, we're close, what was I saying?

PIP

She ran away. Is she okay?

GEORGE

We know she's not dead because she answers texts in rude cryptic
ways.

And I thought—well—I know it's crazy—but I thought maybe if
we sacrificed a deer properly—unlike the duck—if we *consecrated*
a deer—we might be able to get Jenna back. Like a substitution.

A rustling.

GEORGE

A deer!

PIP

No—a bird.

GEORGE

I wonder if it's flying to its nest or away from its nest.

PIP

Away—see her nest there?

GEORGE

What sort of person or bird would abandon her nest to be wild?

George looks at the nest with longing.

PIP

I'm sure she'll come back. George, have a sip of my home brew.
It will calm your nerves.

GEORGE

Okay, thanks.

George drinks from a thermos.

GEORGE

Oh—it's strong.

PIP

Yeah. I think plants are really intelligent, don't you?

George takes another sip.

GEORGE

Mm. Yeah. What is that?

PIP

It's mushroom tea. Just a microdose.

GEORGE

Oh! What's it going to do to me?

PIP

It'll make you insanely happy and super calm.

GEORGE

Oh great.

She takes another sip.

GEORGE

Sometimes I wake up before day breaks, before anyone needs me, and I remember dimly having a relationship with the world beyond people needing me, beyond being a kind of—spigot or drain—and then the kids wake up and my husband wakes up and I forget that somewhere I have a relationship to sky and grass and et cetera. Like now.

PIP

Yeah.

Pip puts an arrow in the bowstring.

GEORGE

The first time you killed a deer—what was it like?

PIP

She was running, and somehow I shot her straight through the heart. She fell, and I ran to her. And I bent down and looked into her eyes and there was still a little bit of grass in her eye. And that moved me so much, this blade of soft grass in her glassy eyes. And then when we took the arrow out, steam rose up out of her. And then Freddie, he skinned her, and then he gave me her heart, and her heart was still warm.

GEORGE

For real life?

PIP

For real life.

GEORGE

And then you ate her?

                                PIP

A little bit at a time. She lasted the whole winter. If you opened
my refrigerator it might seem really gross. Bloody, with animal
organs packed in plastic. Sometimes for breakfast I have a little
ground deer with coconut milk.

                              GEORGE

Oh. That sounds—hm.

A rustling.

                                PIP

Wait—Shh—

                              GEORGE

What?
A deer!

                                PIP

Is it?

                              GEORGE

I think so!

                                PIP

But a small one—maybe a fawn?

                              GEORGE

Oh I hate to kill a fawn—

                                PIP

What's worse, to kill a child or its mother—

                              GEORGE

I don't know—whose grief is worse—the mother or the
child's—oh—

PIP

Shh . . . now is not the time for thinking.
What you want to do is pull back the arrow now.

GEORGE

I'm nervous—

PIP

Just pull back with your arm, get the tension right,
the bow decides when the arrow flies . . .
Not you . . . The bow decides—
You just control your posture—
Stand up straight—pull back, and—
Say a little prayer like:
Gods of the natural world please bring my goddaughter back—

GEORGE

Gods of the natural world please bring my goddaughter back—

PIP

Now say thank you to the deer—

GEORGE

Thank you, deer—

PIP

Now—let go—

George gasps and lets go.
An invisible arrow flies.

Scene 2

George and Pip are in jail.

GEORGE

I didn't know you needed a permit.

PIP

I guess I knew that. Dimly I knew that.

GEORGE

I thought it was just for guns, not for bows and arrows.

PIP

If we'd killed a deer, I'm sure no one would have objected.

GEORGE

Oh my God, a dog, I can't believe I killed a dog. I love dogs. Fuck!

PIP

Yeah.

GEORGE

I need to call the sitter. I'm supposed to pick the kids up from school! I don't see why you can't use cell phones in jail.

PIP

Really?

GEORGE

Jail with cell phones would be much like regular life, people could just sit and not talk to each other and text the outside world. *(Shouting through the bars) Goddammit I need to use the phone!*

PIP

Here let me work on you a little.
It usually takes an hour to get to make a phone call.

GEORGE

Usually?
Fuck! I wonder if they'll press charges.
I would. Family dog.
And the child who saw it die in her arms . . .

Pip starts massaging her.

GEORGE

Oh that's good—thank you . . .
I'm worried Paul will hate me for being in jail.

You know how sometimes your necklaces are tangled up together in a jewelry box, even though you haven't touched them in years, and you think: how on earth did they get tangled? Are they not inanimate objects? How are they moving? I haven't touched them in ten years, how did they wend their way around each other? And I wonder: is that like a marriage? You put these two strands in a box and don't touch them and they're all tangled up together the next time you look?

PIP

You have to take your necklaces out of their boxes every so often to keep them disentangled. You have to take your fingers and pry them apart gently, and hang them loose, side by side.

GEORGE

How?

PIP

Take them out of the box.
Let me just . . . this might hurt a little—

Pip presses a point near George's heart.

PIP

It's a trigger point. Let it go.

GEORGE

Oh!

PIP

You have a lot of stuff buried deep down in there.

GEORGE

Or maybe it's not buried down deep. Maybe it's right on the surface.

Oh! I bet mothers don't hate themselves in *Sweden.*

PIP

Sweden?

GEORGE

We live in a child-hating society that pretends to love children by photographing the babies of English royalty. But actually, they want us behind closed doors, out of the way, alone. We don't know how to feed our children, how to put them to sleep, how to bury our dead. I mean what are you going to pass onto your children, your *individuality?* You make yourself irreplaceable and then you die.

We're supposed to make these humans and replicate something but there is nothing to replicate, nothing which seems obvious and valuable to teach, I mean, how to be an *American* are we going to fucking teach them *that?*

I mean the counterculture, what the hell is that, if we don't have a culture to be counter to—we just work and sleep and order more crap from Amazon. So because you can't give your children *wisdom,* from the *ages,* you say, honey, do you want this crap, or this crap? And they're like: I want *this particular piece of crap.* Other countries have children, we have little relentless live-in *customers*—and we are their fucking patron saints.

Culture is automatically knowing three things to cook that your mother taught you to cook. Culture is knowing how to live and die. Culture is what separates us from the animals. We want someone to tell us *how to live* because we're so sick and tired of making it up as we go along. We just want a slight bit of wisdom passed down through the ages to us, how to make a bowl of soup, how to tie a knot, how to die, et cetera, and *this knowledge is not fucking forthcoming.*

PIP

George.
George.
It's okay.

Pip takes George in her arms.

GEORGE

How did you get so beautiful and so wild?

PIP

I was born that way. So were you.

They kiss.
The sound of keys rattling and footsteps approaching.

GEORGE

Pip—what is that sound?

PIP

Those are keys. And footsteps.
The guard is approaching.
And don't call me Pip in front of the guard.
According to the American legal system, my name is Diana, all right? Diana McKenzie, from Downers Grove, Illinois.

A bright light.

GEORGE

(To the audience) And that's when things began to get really strange. I know—you're saying—things were already fairly strange, weren't they? But at the moment when the guard arrived at our cell, jangling his belt of keys and flashing his flashlight in our eyes, suddenly, Diana, or Pip, looked very afraid, and there was a strange look in her eye, fairly animal.

And when the guard shined his flashlight away from our eyes and opened up the cell, Pip had disappeared, and standing in her place, was a feather. And three small drops of blood.

A feather falls from the ceiling.
George picks it up.

Scene 3

George and Paul at Michael and Jane's house.
It's sort of a mess.
They are all avoiding each other's eyes.

PAUL

Thanks for letting us stay with you.

MICHAEL

It's the least we could do.

JANE

Sorry the house is a bit of a mess . . .

PAUL

Don't worry—

JANE

Are there new signs on your lawn?
Or protesters?

PAUL

Yes. On the lawn. With horrible pictures of mangled animals.
Chanting "dog murderer!"

GEORGE

The children are pretty upset.

JANE

I'm sure.

GEORGE

They ask, "Did you murder a dog, Mommy?" They ask, "If we
got a dog, would you murder it? Can we get a dog?"

JANE

Are you going to get a dog?

PAUL

Not at this moment in time.

GEORGE

Your house makes the kids forget. The finished basement is like
paradise to them. The Ping-Pong table . . .

JANE

You two can have Jenna's room. She won't be sleeping here any-
time soon.

GEORGE

I'm sorry, Jane.

JANE

Anyway . . . I'll get you some towels. And some more blankets for the kids.

GEORGE

Thanks.

Jane exits.
Pause.

MICHAEL

What should we make for dinner?

GEORGE

Oh, let's just order out.

MICHAEL

No! It's the first home-cooked meal you've had since getting out of jail! Let's celebrate.
What are you in the mood for? I'll make it for you.
Sichuan chicken? You used to love my Sichuan chicken.

GEORGE

I'm not really in the mood for *meat*—
Since killing the dog—

MICHAEL

How about a drink? Can I make you a drink?

GEORGE

Sure.

MICHAEL

Gin and tonic? A glass of wine?

GEORGE

Yes! Either—both—sorry I've forgotten how to deal with preferences—

MICHAEL

Don't apologize, I'll get you a drink—

Michael exits.
Paul and George, alone.

GEORGE

Did you sign up for the kids' back-to-school potluck?
I feel like we haven't been very present at school community events lately.

PAUL

We haven't. You've been in jail.

George looks at him.

PAUL

I signed us up for lentils.

GEORGE

Thank you.

Jane comes back in with sheets and a glass of water.

JANE

Here are some fresh sheets and a glass of water.

PAUL AND GEORGE

Thanks.

JANE

Should we, I don't know, play Scrabble?

GEORGE

I'm feeling claustrophobic. I think maybe I'll just take a little walk.

PAUL

By yourself?

GEORGE

Yes.

PAUL

I'm worried about you, George. I don't want you out walking by yourself.

GEORGE

I'll take my phone.

She leaves abruptly.

PAUL

Wow. That was like a physical non sequitur. Like she was here, now she's not.

JANE

How is she?

PAUL

Not great.

JANE

Do you think it's okay, her walking around alone at night?

PAUL

Not really. I'll go after her in ten minutes. How far could she get? It's New Jersey.

JANE

The streetlamps aren't great here. Or the sidewalks. And there are so many deer.

PAUL

Deer aren't dangerous.

JANE

They are during mating season. They charge.

PAUL

Is it mating season?

JANE

Yes.

PAUL

Oh. She'll be okay.
Where is Jenna?

JANE

She's hiding out at a friend's house, from youth orchestra. Her friend's mother is in the Christian right and is offering refuge from her delinquent and highly sexed parents.

PAUL

Ah.

JANE

I keep watching this recording of her first violin concert on my phone—

She plays a recording of a squeaky Bach minuet on her phone, Jenna playing, age eight.
Paul watches it.

JANE

I remember the first time she played a minuet on her small violin I cried. It wasn't her virtuosity, but the idea that for even the unmusical among us, even for the arrhythmic atonal strivers among us, like me, the music is bigger than us and came before us and will go on after us, squeaking away on the smallest violins.

PAUL

Yes.

JANE

She took this enormous breath before she played. This big breath, this small violin, this colossal prayer or hope that the music will continue after we are long gone.

Fuck I miss her, I miss my daughter.

PAUL

Of course you do . . .

JANE

When Jenna was three or four I'd be putting her to sleep and I'd be looking at her, at how beautiful her face was, like some remote Greek sculpture, and she would say: "Don't look at me," and I knew that meant she was about to masturbate with her stuffed animal, so I should leave the room. *Don't look at me*, she said. Parents and children are not supposed to look at one another if there is anything like desire anywhere near.

We screwed up. Not in a moral sense. But in a practical sense. We screwed everything all up.

Jane is about to cry. Paul holds her.

PAUL

She'll come back.

91

Paul holds Jane's face and wipes a tear away.
From a different vantage point, Paul and Jane seem as though they
are about to kiss.
Michael enters.

MICHAEL

How about a little Malbec, vintage—

Jane and Paul look up.

JANE AND PAUL

Hey.

MICHAEL

What's up here?

JANE

Just—sad.

MICHAEL

So that was an "I'm sad" kind of thing I walked in on?

JANE

Right.

MICHAEL

Okay . . . Let's just . . . Rewind. I'm going to walk in the room
again. Hey, how about a little Malbec—I opened it for George.
To celebrate her freedom. Where is she?

JANE

On a walk.

MICHAEL

Who wants a glass?

PAUL

I do.

JANE

I do.

They all drink.

JANE

Oh, I'm sad.

PAUL

I'm worried about George.

MICHAEL

I'm depressed. And slightly angry. I think.

JANE

Fuck.

PAUL

Maybe we should all have sex with each other to make ourselves feel better. Just kidding.

They all laugh wildly.

MICHAEL

That was a weird joke.

A pause.

PAUL

I better go find George.

Paul exits.
Jane and Michael sit for a moment.

JANE

Let's call Jenna again.

MICHAEL

Jane. Are you bored with me?

JANE

No, I'm not bored with you, Jesus, Michael!

MICHAEL

It just seems like—I'm not enough for you—without Jenna.

JANE

Of course it's not fucking enough, Michael, this is not empty nest
syndrome, this is—

MICHAEL

What?

JANE

Hold on—I have to leave a message. Jenna—this is your mother.

*Paul comes in through the door carrying George who has dirt on her
face.*

MICHAEL

George? What happened?

GEORGE

I was in the forest. Looking for Pip. I thought I found her. But it
wasn't her. It was a hawk.

MICHAEL

George are you all right?

Paul wipes the dirt off her face.

GEORGE

I feel a little foggy, like a boat. Maybe we could all go kayaking?

MICHAEL

It's ten o'clock at night.

George drinks a glass of water quickly.
A knock at the door.

MICHAEL

Are you expecting anyone?

JANE

No. I'll get it.

She does. Freddie and David are at the door.

JANE

Hello.

DAVID

Hello.

FREDDIE

Hello.

GEORGE

Oh I was hoping you'd come!

George leaps into Freddie's arms.

GEORGE

Where is Pip?

DAVID

We don't know. In fact that's why we came. She has not been home since the hunting expedition.

JANE   GEORGE

She hasn't?   I told you . . .

DAVID

No. Is she here?

JANE

No!

FREDDIE

Oh. We thought she might be here.

DAVID

Oh, well.

They turn to go.

GEORGE

Don't go!

MICHAEL

Would you like a glass of wine?

DAVID

No thank you.

MICHAEL

Have you called the police?

DAVID

No, Pip doesn't like the police. Sometimes she goes off the grid.

FREDDIE

To clear her head, she says.

DAVID

But she usually comes back within a day or two.

JANE

Did she call you from jail?

FREDDIE

She was in jail?

DAVID

Oh fuck.

PAUL

Was that "oh fuck" as in, "Oh no not again?"

David looks at Freddie.

FREDDIE

Look—she was arrested at a protest years ago. She was in jail, and some bad stuff happened, and when she got out, it was hard for her to get a job having a record, so she changed her name and Social Security number.

MICHAEL

Oh boy.

FREDDIE

So, for the purposes of the law, her name is:

FREDDIE	GEORGE
Diana McKenzie,	Diana McKenzie,
	from Downers Grove, Illinois.
from Downers Grove, Illinois.	

PAUL

So—did she like *steal* a baby's Social Security number?

JANE

Oh Jesus— You can get more than a misdemeanor for identity theft.

DAVID

I don't really believe in identity. Or in individuality.
As you know, Mikhail, I stand with Pythagoras, who said over two thousand years ago: "All things change, but nothing dies: the spirit wanders—passing from beasts into human bodies, or from human spirit to beasts, but never does it perish." You are all so anxious to fix your identities—to walk into Noah's Ark two by two. And then you all wait for it to rain and for the world to end so you can walk out of the ark with a child and remake the universe by getting your adorable children into preschool. Well fuck Noah and his stupid ark.

Freddie and Pip and I walk around the *three* of us, we made a *home.* Maybe it's not clear to you, but I love that woman, I love Diana McKenzie or whatever the hell her name is, it's immaterial. And if she's gone because of you four and your bourgeois fucking fantasies—oh my God—I swear—

FREDDIE

We don't believe in vengeance.

DAVID

I will walk to the ends of the earth to find her. And Freddie will walk with me.

FREDDIE

Yes I will.

DAVID

And when the three of us find each other again we will wrap our limbs around each other and fuck each other so soft and love each other so hard—you would find religion again if you saw us. You spend your little lives praying that nothing illimitable happens to you. But God and love are illimitable. You touched a spark of that fire and I'm afraid you will never be the same. Good luck trying to tame your wild spirits.

Let's go find the woman we love, Freddie.

JANE, MICHAEL, FREDDIE, AND PAUL	GEORGE
Goodbye.	Don't go!

Freddie and David exit, holding hands.

PAUL

Jesus Christ.

JANE

Well that was unexpected.

MICHAEL

I think Dah-veed is right. I think there are—feelings. And those feelings are not being talked about, and are coming out strangely? And if we talked about them—

JANE

No, thanks.

MICHAEL

Jane doesn't like to process her feelings. She finds it vulgar.

JANE

Well, in public.

GEORGE

Do you consider this public?

JANE

It's one of the privileges and honors of adult friendship that you don't have to talk about your feelings. You only have to talk about your feelings with people you're sleeping with—

MICHAEL

But we all did sleep together.

JANE

Yes. And I'd rather not talk about it. We opened the box and now I'd like to *shut it*. And I'm worried about you, George.

MICHAEL

Well I think we should talk about it. I think it might help George. I've been rereading *The Ethical Slut*—

JANE

Oh no—

MICHAEL

And it says, to be an ethical slut—

Jane groans.

MICHAEL

—you have to talk about your feelings—or it all goes pear shaped—and it says there's this feeling you can cultivate, called compersion—

JANE

Oh my God, what a horrible word—

PAUL

Compersion?

MICHAEL

It's taking pleasure in your lover taking pleasure—

JANE

I hate the word lover—and the word caress—and the word
moist—and the word *panties*. And I hate all words that have been
made up in the last twelve years and added to the dictionary—
like compersion—

MICHAEL

But forget *the word*—what about the concept—did you all experience compersion, that night?

She looks around.

MICHAEL

Jane, did you have compersion?

JANE

I can't remember.

MICHAEL

Paul, did you have compersion?

PAUL

Yes. I think so.

MICHAEL

Say more.

PAUL

I saw a look of ecstasy on George's face and I believe it turned
me on.

GEORGE

(To Paul) Really? I remember a look in your eyes, a look in your eyes that terrified me, and Jane was holding Dah-veed in her hands when Jenna walked in—

MICHAEL

David?

PAUL

David?

JANE

That wasn't David's, that was—

GEORGE

What? Whose?

JANE

David and Pip and Freddie went home. At midnight. Freddie wanted to drive before the roads got full of drunk people.

GEORGE

What? No they didn't. We had a massive sevensome.

PAUL

No George. We had a massive foursome.

GEORGE

If that wasn't David's whose was it?

MICHAEL

Paul's.

GEORGE

I'm losing my mind.

JANE

There were hash brownies.

GEORGE

Yes but—Pip—the slender fingers—it was Pip—wasn't it? Who
was it?

JANE

That was me.

GEORGE

Oh!

MICHAEL

Pip wasn't there.

GEORGE

So it was us, it was us all along?

PAUL

Yes.

GEORGE

Oh, God.
(To Paul) That was yours, in Jane's hand?

Paul nods.

GEORGE

I want to go home.
No, I want to go to the forest. No.
We are just vessels and it all goes through us truly.
It's really very confusing, the eating, the wanting, the flesh. I'm
not a puritan, or a pilgrim. It's just—maybe I want to give up and
work with abandoned dogs.

PAUL

Honey?

GEORGE

And God, the whole idea of us eating God for communion, what if it's the other way around? And we are all part of his body already. Because how else do you account for omniscience? Maybe we are all the cells in his body, we are all traveling through rivers of blood to get to God where we were all along.

JANE

Honey, do you have a fever?

Jane feels George's forehead.

GEORGE

And you know what really irks me, Jane? If we're really going to talk about our feelings?

JANE

What is it?

GEORGE

That you skinny-dipped with my high school boyfriend Arthur when we were seventeen. And you held his hand in the water. *After* you dropped me off. Because you said you were scared of drowning. Because that's how your grandfather died.

JANE

That is how he died.

GEORGE

But come on—so you had to hold Arthur's hand naked? Because of your dead grandfather?

JANE

You're still thinking about this?

GEORGE

Yes.

JANE

I'm sorry.

GEORGE

Thank you.

MICHAEL

Come on. Arthur? Who cares about Arthur? Why can't we talk about us?

Pause.

GEORGE

When we were in this living room, on New Year's Eve, I saw Paul looking at you, Jane—and I can't unsee how he saw you.

JANE

He looked at me?

GEORGE

Yes. He looked at you. *Like he loves you.*
And I thought, Paul loves you. But then I thought: of course Paul loves Jane. Just like I love Michael. And you love me.
Paul do you love Jane?

PAUL

Yes, of course.

GEORGE

Of course. Jane do you love Paul?

JANE

Yes.

GEORGE

Michael do you love me?

MICHAEL

Yes.

GEORGE

But like this?

George kisses Michael.

GEORGE

Or like this?

George kisses Michael differently.

GEORGE

Or like this?

George kisses Jane.

GEORGE

Or like this?

George kisses Jane differently.

GEORGE

Michael do you love Paul?

MICHAEL

Yes.

GEORGE

But how?

Michael and Paul kiss.
This time the kissing is not like a wild orgy.
They kiss and it's about forgiveness and love.

GEORGE

Can it get bigger than two people? Can it? Can it include other
people?
Otherwise it's so small! Oh my life is so small! Can this *(She ges-*
tures to the space between her and Paul) include the world? I can't—
hold it.

PAUL

George—

GEORGE

I want—I want—it's not compersion—in Latin, it's *caritas.*

JANE

What does it mean?

GEORGE

It's like, it's like—do you know the passage—Paul?

PAUL

No.

GEORGE

No not the passage, Paul, the passage by Paul?

PAUL

I think you're the only Catholic here, George.

GEORGE

It's something like:
Love is patient, love is kind, love does not envy, love is not puffed
up, love does not parade itself around.
Prophecies fail. Knowledge goes. Love stays.

PAUL

You are so fucking Catholic, George.

GEORGE

"Fucking" as a modifier for Catholic is little hostile—

PAUL

Sorry—you are incurably Catholic, George.

GEORGE

So?

PAUL

What am I going to do with you?

GEORGE

Love me.

PAUL

Done.

GEORGE

Not done, doing.

PAUL

You want me to conjugate my love for you?

GEORGE

Yes.

PAUL

In front of them?

GEORGE

In front of everyone.

PAUL

I'm not a good conjugator. You're the conjugator.

She looks at him.

PAUL

Amo, amas . . .
George, I've been so lonely.

GEORGE

Me too.

A breath.
It's hard for Paul.
It is as though they get married again,
in front of new witnesses.

PAUL

I have loved,
I will love,
And I love you, George.

They embrace.

MICHAEL

Can we—I don't know—can we *sing* something together—I
mean—like maybe we shouldn't all be *fucking* each other all the
time but maybe we could form like a *band* or something?

JANE

Michael?

MICHAEL

I'll get my guitar.

JANE

I'll come with you.

They exit.
Paul and George have a silent and tender moment together.
Jane and Michael reenter with a guitar.

MICHAEL

What should we sing?

GEORGE

What do we all know?

MICHAEL

How about the song I sang at your anniversary party?

GEORGE

The one you made up? Yes please.

MICHAEL

It goes a little something like this . . .

Michael sings the following song.
If others can sing, they might join in.

MICHAEL

(Singing)
    A little box of days
    spent together
    married.

And what is it to be married?
Well—

Married is: A day
at Cora's Café
you say:
You're a good wife, am I a
Good husband?

Yes, I say.
And then we swim.
Married is: We talk about our
Bodies
you tell me

what's in your stomach
and we
talk of itchy bumps.
Married is: You come home
My eye is hurt and you come fast
And put a warm towel on me.

And married is:
Jenna runs
Between us

so much
Joy on her face
and it is your face
and it is my face
and it is her face
and she runs.

And the smell of apples in winter.

They finish the song.

JANE

Let's all get married.

GEORGE

Yes, let's all get married.

PAUL

Um—

A clatter.
A knock at the window.
A showering of feathers.

JANE

Look!

MICHAEL

Oh my God!

GEORGE

Pip! It's Pip!
You came back!
She came back!

PAUL

Should I get a—

JANE

A what?

PAUL

I don't know—a broom?

MICHAEL

Should I open a window, she'll fly out again . . .

GEORGE

See it's Pip, I kept her feather, see it matches, Pip!

George pulls out a feather from her pocket and compares.

GEORGE

She's injured, look!
Oh, get some milk!
Or a blanket!
A bandage?
What do birds eat?

PAUL

Worms.

GEORGE

Quick, get a worm!
She seems nervous
And excited—

Jane cradles the bird in her palm.

JANE

I think she's about to lay an egg, oh, an egg in my palm?

The bird lays an egg in Jane's palm.

JANE

Oh my God she just laid an egg in my palm.
I have to stay perfectly still . . .

PAUL

What is going on?

MICHAEL

A bird birth—

JANE

Oh my God she's laying another egg. Help help—

MICHAEL

What is she? Why isn't she going to her nest?

GEORGE

Because it's Pip!

The doorbell rings.

PAUL

Jesus Christ.

MICHAEL

I'll get it!

JANE

She laid another egg—three eggs in my palm! Someone come hold her. I'm going to drop them!

Jenna is at the door.
She walks in.

MICHAEL

Jenna! Oh honey! You came back!

JANE

Jenna!

JENNA

They're still here?
Seriously? They're still here?
And why is there a fucking bird in here? Did you get a *pet* when I left? To replace me? That's sick! Goodbye!

MICHAEL

Jenna! No—it's not our bird—it just flew in through the window—

JANE

Stay, honey!

JENNA

What's wrong with their house?

JANE

Animal rights activists—

JENNA	MICHAEL
Animal rights—	It's not worth going into—
	We're just so glad you're home,
	honey!

JENNA

Wait, are they staying in *my room?*

JANE

(To Jenna) It's not permanent . . . *(To her friends)* Is it?

JENNA

Jesus I come back and they're in my fucking bed? Where am I? Is this my home? There are animals . . . and . . . Mom, why are you holding three eggs in your hands?

JANE

The bird laid them there . . . Michael, can you hold them?

MICHAEL

(Taking the eggs) Uh, sure . . .

JENNA

I'm leaving.

GEORGE

Jenna, we'll go. Of course we wouldn't have taken over your bedroom if we'd known you were coming home. We'll just wake the kids and put them in the car.

She turns back.

JENNA

The kids are here too?

GEORGE

Yes. Sleeping.

JENNA

So you weren't all about to have another orgy?

MICHAEL

No! But if we were, you have no right to judge us.

JENNA   JANE

Dad!   Michael!

JANE

George has been in jail. She just got home.

JENNA

Auntie George? In jail? Why?

GEORGE

I murdered a dog by accident.

MICHAEL

How'd you get home?

JENNA

Amtrak.

PAUL

I love Amtrak.

JANE

(To Jenna) Why?

JENNA

Eisa and I had a fight.

JANE

Oh? What about?

GEORGE

We'll leave.

JENNA

Auntie George please just stay. Who cares it's all so fucked up anyway. Eisa called me a slut.

JANE

A slut, why?

JENNA

She found my birth control.

JANE

You're on birth control?

JENNA

Mom. Come on.

GEORGE

(To the audience) And time and space collapsed and Jenna was actually Jane when I first met her, when we were seventeen. I blinked and my seventeen-year-old best friend Jane was a litigator with

aging elbows and her daughter was nubile, fierce, and on birth control. Time was running rampant and we were all victim-observers. They talked and talked and there were accusations along the lines of:

JENNA

Mom, when I walked in you had Paul's *dick* in your hand and Dad was taking Auntie George from behind I mean how is that supposed to make me feel—

GEORGE

And other things were said like:

JANE

How dare you not return our phone calls how dare you *abscond*—

MICHAEL

—we were so worried, honey—

JANE

—we called the police we called private detectives this has nothing to do with our sex lives—

JENNA	JANE
This has everything to do with your sex life—	This has to do with you punishing us —*just because we exist*—

JANE

And who are you sleeping with on that birth control—

MICHAEL

Let's not, let's not go there—

JANE

are you sleeping with that little twit on the debate team—

JENNA

(Overlapping) Aaagh—

JANE

—I don't care about the sex but you could get HPV if you're not using a condom; basically all men right now are walking genital warts—

JENNA

I took Sex Ed, Mom, I know about genital warts—

JANE

I thought you were a virgin! I thought you would tell me if you ever—

JENNA

Mom you're so naive—

JANE

Well then why shouldn't *we* have sex if you're having sex—

JENNA

It's fine for you to have sex with *Dad* I just don't want to see it—

JANE

It's no fair, no fair, you have to become an animal in order to have children and then you have a child and you have to disguise your animal nature forever after—

Jane weeps.

JANE

Jenna, I'm sorry.

What can I say? *(As in: Come home to me)*

JENNA
(As in: I will come home to you) Mom.

Mother and daughter embrace.

POSTLUDE

Time changes and George turns to the audience.
Back to the forest, the living room now a dream.

GEORGE

(To the audience) I took the eggs. And I put them in a makeshift
nest. Maybe all nests are makeshift. Temporary. Handmade. Used
until the cared-for outgrow their usage. And we stayed at Jane
and Michael's until the animal rights protesters were gone. And
one day the bird flew away. And one day the eggs hatched. And
the mother bird didn't come back to feed them. And so the chicks
died, one by one. And it was sad. And my children and I had a
funeral and planted them in the ground.

Jenna over time forgave us. I went back to being Auntie George
and I helped her with college applications. And the trauma of see-
ing her parents' aberrant sex lives up close—it became an anec-

dote in a college application. It helped her get into Bennington. She wrote: "And I came to accept the spirit inside the flesh that were my parents. And in accepting that they had bodies, I came to accept that I too was embodied, and limited by the perceptions of my own flesh."

Pip came home one day too. Bedraggled and thirsty and trailing feathers, she came home to Freddie and David in human form, who welcomed her and nursed her back to health.

My own children grew up too. My marriage survived their childhood. Our lifelong friends stayed our lifelong friends until our deathbed, I think. I don't know because I haven't died yet. None of us has. It seems like you have omniscience when you can talk to the audience in a play but I don't have omniscience because I haven't died yet. But when I do die I want my three best friends there. And I want there to be singing. I would want my best friends to take my husband into their arms, and comfort him.

I once knew a woman who was terminally ill so she helped her husband learn to cook all the favorite meals she had prepared for him in life. She taught him each meal, one by one, as she was dying. How to roast a chicken. How to make spaghetti Bolognese. And I thought—love. To care more about your meals continuing to be cooked—for the bellies of those you have cherished—than you care about your own future absence.

Music and food, and love, carrying on after, unmade by any one single person. Like this—

The sound of Bach's minuet being played on a small violin.

GEORGE

That's my daughter playing. And then another violin is added, in counterpoint—a duet—

Another violin is added—

GEORGE

In love we think all we can tolerate is a duet—but then another violin is added—A trio—

Another—

GEORGE

And then—a quartet—each with its own beauty and on and on—

And I can no longer hear my daughter playing, but the melody is still there—and more and more children play—until three hundred violins are all playing together in one church.

And the sound cannot be contained.

And oh my God we're all straining so hard for transcendence, and there it was all along.

More violins are added.
If possible, one hundred children onstage are revealed playing the violin together in the forest.
A bird flies.

THE END

Afterword

On happy endings

Happy endings are not in vogue.

Happy endings are a compound noun now used to describe unseemly behavior in massage parlors. Dramatically, ambivalent endings are perhaps more fashionable—the equivalent of a character hopping on one foot as the lights go down.

Playwrights might be wary of happy endings because these are not happy times. Or maybe we are wary of happy endings because we are wary in the contemporary theater of unmixed genres—a full-out comedy, or a full-on tragedy. In Shakespeare, comedies end happily with a marriage, and tragedies end with a body pileup. But undiluted genres are more the province of Hollywood, not theater.

So it was with some trepidation that I put the word "happy" in a title.

Is the search for happiness stage-worthy? Aristotle talked of *eudaimonia*, the good life. This is a search for the good for its own sake. That seems a worthy topic for philosophy, but is it a worthy topic for drama: how to live? Weddings are the traditional endings for comedies going back to the Greeks, but being married and having children does not end anyone's searching, though it implies an end in many narrative structures. Can a play start at the happy middle and go forward?

Tolstoy said, "All happy families are alike; each unhappy family is unhappy in its own way." And so Tolstoy furthered the myth of unhappiness as a marker of uniqueness. What if happy endings are also unique unto themselves; and each search to find them as rare and singular as the proverbial snowflake?

. . .

I have friends that are like family, and who challenge the notion that a nuclear family is complete unto itself. Perhaps nowhere more than in America do we persist in the fiction that we can get absolutely everything we need from the nuclear family and from our spouses; our great-aunts unknown—our parents flung across the country—our neighbors who we have never met. When one tries to raise children in that cloistered, closed environment, something frays, and I believe that something is often the mother.

Plays with motherhood at the center, written by mothers, are quite new. We've only had them for the last twenty or thirty years. Our first woman playwright in the English language, Aphra Behn—a poet, a playwright, and a spy—did not have children. Lorraine Hansberry was the godmother to Nina Simone's daughter, but did not have her own children. Lillian Hellman—no children. Between Aphra Behn's death in 1689 we would have to wait almost three hundred years to read plays by women who happen to have children—among the first were Tina Howe, Adrienne Kennedy, and Marsha Norman. We had to wait even longer to hear from women critics with children writing about plays written by women with children. We must be unembarrassed and unashamed to write from our experience, knowing that we are reaching each other without sometimes ever speaking to one another.

In ancient Greek there are three words for love. *Eros* is sexual, "an intermediary between gods and humans"; *agape* is a full empathetic love of humanity—which is similar to the Latin word *caritas*, "from charity." And *storge* is affection between parents and children. *How to transcend a happy marriage* is ultimately a meditation on those three kinds of love.

Boundless love! Specific love! Love bigger than romantic love. I was so intrigued, when doing research, to discover that Pythagoras believed in metempsychosis, a theory of the soul in which the soul is immortal and passes through cycles of incarnation. Pythagoras might have borrowed his ideas from Hindu philosophy. And then they made their way into Shakespeare's *As You Like It*, which has shades of Ovid, and Ovid includes Pythagoras in *Metamorphoses*.

I won't parse these sources endlessly, but I might direct you to them while you're thinking about or working on the play.

I'll leave you with the words of George:

GEORGE

Can it get bigger than two people? Can it? Can it include other people?
Otherwise it's so small! Oh my life is so small! Can this *(She gestures to the space between her and Paul)* include the world? I can't—hold it.

—*Sarah Ruhl*
New York
2019

Acknowledgments

I'D LIKE TO THANK the writers of *The Ethical Slut*, Dossie Easton and Janet Hardy. I have so much gratitude toward the brave and wonderful actors at Lincoln Center: the beautiful Marisa, Lena, Brian, Omar, David, Austin, Naian, Robin. In addition to that divine cast, some actors who helped me greatly in the development of the play are: Rachel Weisz, Jessica Hecht, Adina Verson, Michael Esper, Marianne Rendón, Dylan Baker, Sandra Oh, Michael Cerveris, Danny Jenkins, and Anthony Edwards. Rachel—thank you for the title. For his magic, I would like to thank Alexander Boyce. For his transcendent music, Todd Almond. For fourteen years of beautiful collaboration—I thank Rebecca Taichman. Thanks to my dear friends Luke and Mindy. And to my husband Tony who I wrote this play for.

Married Is

Music by Todd Almond
Lyrics by Sarah Ruhl

Freely

MICHAEL: A lit-tle box of days spent to-geth-er mar-ried.

And what is it to be___ mar-ried?___ Well-

Unhurried; with rubato

Mar - ried is: a day___ at Cor - a's___ Caf - é. You say:

you're a good___ wife,___ am I___ a good hus - band? Yes, I say.___ And then we

swim.

Mar - ried is: We talk___ a-bout our bod - ies.___ you tell me

Music preparation by Mark Wurzelbacher - mwurzelb@gmail.com

ZACH DEZON

SARAH RUHL is a playwright, poet, and essayist. Her plays include *How to transcend a happy marriage*; *For Peter Pan on her 70th birthday*; *Becky Nurse of Salem*; *The Oldest Boy*; *In the Next Room or the vibrator play* (Pulitzer Prize finalist, Tony Award nominee for Best Play); *The Clean House* (Susan Smith Blackburn Prize, Pulitzer Prize finalist); *Passion Play* (PEN America Award, Fourth Freedom Forum Playwriting Award from The Kennedy Center); adaptations of Woolf's *Orlando* and Chekhov's *Three Sisters*; *Late: a cowboy song*; *Melancholy Play*; *Dear Elizabeth*; *Dead Man's Cell Phone* (Helen Hayes Award); *Eurydice*; and *Stage Kiss*. Her plays have been produced on Broadway at the Lyceum Theatre by Lincoln Center; Off-Broadway at Playwrights Horizons, Second Stage Theater, and at Lincoln Center's Mitzi Newhouse Theater. Her plays have been produced all over the country and internationally. They have been translated into more than twelve languages. Ms. Ruhl received her MFA from Brown University where she studied with Paula Vogel. She has received the Steinberg Distinguished Playwright Award, the Susan Smith Blackburn Prize, the Whiting Award, the Lilly Award, a PEN/Laura Pels Award for American Playwright in Mid-career, and a MacArthur Fellowship. Her book of essays, *100 Essays I Don't Have Time to Write* (Faber and Faber) was a *New York Times* Notable Book of the Year. A book of correspondence with poet Max Ritvo, *Letters from Max: a book of friendship*, was published by Milkweed Editions. A book of essays, *What My Phone Won't Teach Me and Other Essays* (TCG), and a book of poetry, *44 Poems for You* (Copper Canyon Press), are forthcoming. She teaches at the Yale School of Drama and lives in Brooklyn with her family.